The Journey of the Monarch

by Isabella Cummings

illustrated by Christine Joy Pratt

Harcourt

Orlando   Boston   Dallas   Chicago   San Diego

Visit *The Learning Site!*

www.harcourtschool.com

In the early fall, the leaves had begun to change color. Spectators came to the zoo to see both the animals and the changing leaves.

As the days grew colder, the giraffes and elephants spent more time indoors. The polar bears, however, were overjoyed to have cold weather. They stood their ground and refused to go indoors.

People stood outside, too. They bundled up in warm overcoats and watched the animals.

Any time of year is a good time to go to the zoo. In the winter, the animals do different things.

High in the bright sky, a huge group of monarch butterflies flew over the zoo. The United States winter would be too cold for them. They flew off to find hospitality in a warmer place.

Some of the monarchs were only two or three weeks old. They would go on the long journey, too. The monarchs were flying to Mexico. There the warmer air would welcome them for the winter.

Making this trip is quite a feat. Some monarchs travel more than 1,500 miles!

As the monarchs fly south, others
join them on their journey to Mexico.
Millions of monarchs fill the skies in
an unending line.

The monarchs fly about 50 miles each day. Then they stop to rest on tree branches or flowers. Every day they continue flying. They are unstoppable.

Monarch butterflies sip nectar from flowers. It is hard to believe, but they gain weight during their trip! The fat in their bodies gives them energy to fly. The strong winds help them on their way, too.

After many weeks, more than one hundred million monarch butterflies will arrive in the Mexican mountains. Some will return to the same tree they lived in the year before!

In the Mexican mountains, it is cool, but not cold. During the day it gets warmer than the United States.

For five or six months, the monarchs stay in Mexico. When spring arrives, each hero and heroine makes the long journey back to his or her northern home.